JEWS and "JEWISH CHRISTIANITY"

JEWS and "JEWISH CHRISTIANITY"

by

DAVID BERGER
and
MICHAEL WYSCHOGROD

KTAV PUBLISHING HOUSE, INC.
1978

Library of Congress Cataloging in Publication Data

Berger, David, 1943-
  Jews and "Jewish Christianity".

  Bibliography: p.
  1. Judaism—Apologetic works. 2. Jewish Christians.
3. Missions to Jews. I. Wyschogrod, Michael, joint author. II. Title.
BM648.B45   296.3   78-9423
ISBN 0-87068-675-5

MANUFACTURED IN THE UNITED STATES OF AMERICA

CONTENTS

PREFACE

The Jewish Community Relations Council of New York serves as the central coordinating body on issues of concern to the Jewish community in the metropolitan area. Recognizing the increase in missionary activity directed at Jews, the JCRC established a Task Force on Missionary Activity to alert and educate the Jewish community and to develop appropriate responses.

Early on, the Task Force Subcommittee on Publications recognized the need for a work that would present a reasoned discussion of the major issues in readable fashion. We are therefore proud to have served as the catalytic agent which led to the writing of *Jews and "Jewish Christianity"* by two distinguished specialists in this field.

It is our hope that this publication will contribute to a better understanding of the relevant issues and that it will deepen the Jewish community's commitment to the crucial task of furthering Jewish education.

Seymour P. Lachman
Chairman, JCRC Task Force
on Missionary Activity

111 West 40th Street
New York, N. Y. 10018

A Note to the Reader

This booklet has been written for two purposes: first, to persuade Jews who have been attracted by "Jewish Christianity" to take another look at the issues; second, to familiarize other readers with a Jewish approach to what has become a controversial and hotly debated topic. The introduction and final word are addressed specifically to the first group; other readers can skip them and concentrate on the substantive discussions which constitute the bulk of the work.

1 INTRODUCTION

You were born a Jew. You may have gone to Hebrew school for some years and had a *Bar Mitzva* or a *Bat Mitzva*. Whether you had a good Jewish education, a poor one, or none at all, you are now a teenager, in your twenties, thirties, or any age. And you have a problem.

Your problem is Jesus of Nazareth. For a long time, he meant nothing to you. You knew that you were a Jew and Jews didn't believe in Jesus. But at some point that began to change. You may have read something or heard a speaker say that you cannot be saved unless you accept Jesus as your personal savior and, furthermore, that you can remain a good Jew and accept Jesus. In fact, you may have been told, to accept Jesus as your savior made you a fulfilled or Messianic Jew. Perhaps for the first time in your life you met sincerely religious people who reached out to welcome you and include you into a real fellowship. You were probably told that only through Jesus could your sins be forgiven. You then read portions of the New Testament and you were moved by the personality of Jesus: his love of God and his fellow man, and his compassion for the weak and suffering. And you are now in the process of becoming a Jewish Christian, or maybe you already have become one or are just beginning to think of becoming a Jewish Christian. Or your situation may be different from anything described so far. But you are a Jew and are attracted to Jesus and Jewish Christianity.

This booklet is for you. It was written in a spirit of reverence. Chances are very good that if you have begun thinking about becoming a Jewish Christian you have encountered some hostility from Jewish relatives and friends. Some of them may have had little Jewish commitment until they heard about your Jewish Christianity, at which point they berated you for apostasy, being disloyal to your people, and other nasty things. To you, all this sounded very unfair, because you did not think you were being disloyal to anybody, just happy with a newly found faith. And so you may be confused. Can I be a Jew and a Christian? Why has Judaism rejected Christianity? These and other questions come to your mind. You have heard these questions answered by your new Christian friends. But since you are a fair person, you want to hear the other side of the case. But you want to hear it from a Jew who knows what he is talking about and who won't abuse you and call you names. After you have heard both sides of the story, you will make up your own mind, and this is as it should be, because every person is responsible for his own choices, whether right or wrong.

The purpose of this booklet is to explain the Jewish point of view with respect to Jews becoming Christians or Jewish Christians. Judaism never did and does not wish to discourage gentiles (those who are not Jews) from becoming or remaining Christians. The reason for this, as you will see, is that Judaism has never believed that everybody should become Jewish. From the Jewish point of view, good people of all religions have a share in the world to come. Judaism does, however, believe that Jews should be Jews and nothing else. The purpose of this booklet is therefore to explain why Jews ought not to become Christians or Jewish Christians, but it is not directed at anyone who is not Jewish.

This booklet was written in a spirit of respect for those to whom it is addressed. We assume that you are a sincere seeker of the truth and that your search is a genuinely religious one. It is necessary to say this because often Jews who speak to fellow Jews attracted to Christianity find it hard to believe that such Jewish Christians are sincere. The reason for this is simple. For many centuries many Jews who converted to Christianity did so out of motives of self-interest rather than religious sincerity. Up to very recent times, being a Jew in a Christian world was a social and economic disadvantage. Many occupations were closed to Jews, as were the fancier social circles. Many Jews who embraced Christianity, therefore, acted out of self-interest rather than genuine religious conviction, and Jews resented such conversions of convenience, as did sincere Christians. Gradually, this attitude became deeply ingrained in the Jewish mind, and as a result many Jews find it hard to believe that a Jew who embraces Christianity can be sincere.

But times do change. While discrimination against Jews has by no means disappeared, it has diminished, particularly in the United States. Today, in this country, most Jews who move toward Christianity do not do so out of social or economic self-interest. They must therefore be addressed with the respect that any sincere person who seeks truth deserves. And that is the spirit in which this booklet was written. In addition to respect, the Jew who has been attracted to Christianity also deserves honesty. We will not hide our goal. It is to retrieve for Judaism every possible Jew. We will attempt to do so honestly and with love, and with the knowledge that, in the final analysis, each person is responsible only to God for the decisions he makes.

One more word about motivation. Nowadays, many Jews who hear about Jews involved with Christianity attribute such involvement to lack of Jewish education and/or psychological problems. It is true that many Jews, both old and young, lack a proper Jewish education. And it is also true that many persons today have psychological problems. But religious choices can rarely be explained just on psychological grounds. In one way or another, a person is responding to God and to spiritual realities. The spiritual realm involves man's soul, and that is deeper than the mind that the psychologist can understand. There will be no attempt here to "explain away" your interest in Christianity by reducing it to a psychological or educational problem. If your Jewish education is weak, then you ought to improve it, and this booklet will play a small role in so doing. But above all, you can be sure that you are being taken seriously on a religious and spiritual level.

There is one more important point that must be made before we begin to discuss the issues. To a certain extent, throughout our discussion we will be "proving" things or trying to show that the "proofs" offered by others leave something to be desired. As you read on, and especially if you pay careful attention to the various "proofs" offered, you might come to the conclusion that we consider religious beliefs to be based purely on rational proofs. But that is not our intention. Religious beliefs are to a large extent based on faith, and this is true of both the Jewish and the Christian believer. Let us look at some specific examples.

Much of the debate between Judaism and Christianity involves the interpretation of passages from the Bible. To the believing Jew, the Hebrew Bible, or Old Testament in Christian terminology, is the word of God. To the believing Christian, both the Old and New Testaments are divinely inspired. Now the belief that a particular book is or is not the word of God cannot be proven objectively. Such a belief is held by faith, and Christians speak of faith as something given by God as a gift to some and not to others. The encounter between Judaism and Christianity is, to some extent, an encounter of different faith positions, and honest Jews and Christians should recognize this fact. This is true not only with regard to the question of whether or not the New Testament is divinely inspired but also of a number of other questions, such as the divinity of Jesus and under what circumstances God forgives sins. Faith plays an important part in both Judaism and Christianity, and it would be less than forthright for either Jews or Christians to assert that they can prove their case beyond doubt and therefore do not require faith.

But what is faith? Is it simply believing things without any evidence? Is anyone entitled to believe anything simply on the grounds of faith without having to give any reason for his beliefs? This is a difficult question to answer and theologians have written a great deal about it. Perhaps the best example of faith is that of Abraham, about whom the Bible says (Genesis 15:6): "Abram put his faith in the Lord, and the Lord counted that faith to him as righteousness." It is important to note the context in which this verse appears. The verse appears in connection with Abraham's puzzlement about God's reliability. God had promised Abraham that his offspring would be as many as the dust of the earth. And then Abraham and Sarah had no children. After Sarah passed her menopause, it looked as if God was not going to keep his promise. It is at this point that we are told of Abraham's faith. Abraham believed that God would keep his promise even though, from the human point of view, it didn't look at all likely. This sort of trusting faith is somewhat different from the believing sort that we have in mind when we speak of faith in God's existence or the divine inspiration of Scripture; nevertheless, it shows that faith has an element of trusting someone in spite of the existence of contrary evidence. If we truly love God and feel his love for us, we trust him to keep his promises and to do what is good for us.

At the same time, it cannot be the will of God that human beings act irrationally. Even if things held on faith cannot be proven with certainty, there is much that can be understood. Take something like interpreting the meaning of the Bible. In order to understand the Bible we have to read it. Those who cannot read Hebrew or Greek have to depend on translations, and translators often disagree about the correct translation of certain passages. Furthermore, when reading anything written many centuries ago, we have to be sure we understand the expressions and way of thinking of the people to whom the work was addressed.

Otherwise we are in danger of misunderstanding its message.

This is particularly true of historical religions like Judaism and Christianity, whose claims to credibility are based on happenings in time and place. These religions have long histories during which certain ideas developed. Take something like the idea of the Messiah. It is really impossible to understand the meaning of the claim that someone was the Messiah without understanding what the idea meant among ancient Jews and how it came to mean what it did. Christianity was born within Judaism. Jesus and his disciples were all Jews. They were educated along Jewish lines and thought of themselves as Jews. To understand Christianity, it is therefore necessary to know a good deal about Judaism. And this is particularly true for a Jew who becomes interested in Christianity. He has to face the Jewish roots of Christianity and therefore his own Jewishness, which is something he may never have really examined before.

We will attempt to explain how Judaism views Christianity and why it cannot agree with some of the most important Christian beliefs. Because we will concentrate on areas of disagreement, we may give the impression that there are no areas of agreement. That is, of course, not so. Belief in the dignity of man as created in the image of God is one area of agreement. So is the teaching that we must help those less fortunate because God so desires it. And there are many other areas of agreement. Nevertheless, for a Jew to come to believe that Jesus was God—to take one idea in Christianity that Judaism cannot accept—is a very serious matter, and so we hope you will read on with an open mind.

2 JESUS AND THE MESSIAH

Let us begin with the fundamental belief that Jesus was —and is—the Messiah. Since the very word *Christ* means Messiah, this belief lies at the heart of the Christian faith. But how do we go about testing the claim that Jesus was the Messiah? The first thing to remember is that the term *Messiah* gets its basic meaning from Biblical prophecy; it is only because of such prophecy that people expected the Messiah in the first place. Any person claiming to be the Messiah must, therefore, be able to pass a very exacting test: Has he done what the Bible expects of the Messiah?

We must begin, then, by taking a look at the Bible as a whole. How would the Messiah of the Hebrew Bible be described by someone who had just read the text for the first time without any knowledge of either Judaism or Christianity? If our hypothetical friend were a perceptive reader, his first observation would be that the word *messiah* simply refers to any king or high priest who was anointed with oil in accordance with the custom of ancient Israel. There is, however, a rather special king from the House of David who is described in several Biblical passages as the man who will preside over a redeemed and perfected world. Eventually, Jews came to use the word *Messiah* (this time the capital *M* is justifiable) to refer to that king, and it is in this context that any man claiming to be the Messiah must be judged.

In other words, the only way to define "the Messiah" is as the king who will rule during what we call the Messianic age. The central criterion for evaluating a Messiah must therefore be a single question: Has the Messianic age come? It is only in terms of this question that "the Messiah" means anything. What, then, does the Bible say about the Messianic age? Here is a brief description by a famous Christian scholar: "The recovery of independence and power, an era of peace and prosperity, of fidelity to God and his law, of justice and fair-dealing and brotherly love among men, and of personal rectitude and piety" (G. F. Moore, *Judaism,* II, p. 324). If we think about this sentence just for a moment in light of the history of the last two thousand years, we will begin to see what enormous obstacles must be overcome if we are to believe in the messianic mission of Jesus. If Jesus was the Messiah, why have suffering and evil continued and even increased in the many centuries since his death?

We don't know much about Messianic figures between the period of the Hebrew Bible and the lifetime of Jesus. The first Christian century, however, was a time when tensions between Jews and Romans were reaching the boiling point, and we know of at least three or four "Messiahs" during that century. In that sense, Jesus' career was not unique; it reflected a fairly common tendency in Jewish society at that time. In fact, at least one of the other Messiahs was also killed by the Romans. Unlike the other movements, the one started by Jesus survived its founder. The direction that Christianity took differed from what Jesus had in mind (as we shall see, he would have protested his designation as God with every fiber of his being), and it is very important to understand how the belief that Jesus was the Messiah survived his death.

In light of what was universally understood to be the function of the Messiah, the crucifixion was a terrible logical and psychological blow to Jesus' followers. The Messiah was supposed to redeem Israel, bring peace and justice to the world, make the wolf live peacefully with the lamb, and see to it that "they learn war no more" (Isaiah 2:1–4, 11:1–10). Something, it seemed, had gone terribly wrong. How could the paradox of a crucified Messiah be explained?

A story is told about a modern rabbi and a Christian missionary which highlights this problem. One of the great rabbis of the last hundred years was riding on a train in Russia, and he overheard a conversation between a Christian missionary and some deeply religious but uneducated Jews. The Jews had just expressed their confidence in the judgment of the ancient rabbis concerning the Messiah. "In that case," asked the Christian, "how can you explain the fact that Rabbi Akiva [one of the greatest Talmudic rabbis] initially thought that Bar Kochba [a Jewish revolutionary of the second century] was the Messiah?" The Jews were taken aback and could find no answer. The rabbi, who had been listening quietly, turned to the Christian and asked, "How do you know that Bar Kochba wasn't the Messiah?" "That's obvious," he replied; "Bar Kochba was killed without bringing the redemption."

There can be little doubt that many of the first-century Jews who had been attracted by Jesus' preaching sadly submitted to the conclusion forced upon them by his death. They had been mistaken. God had not yet chosen to redeem his people. They would have to wait once more, however long it might take, however much their hearts might be aching for redemption.

But for others this was impossible. The belief was too strong, the hurt too great, to face the terrible truth. There simply had to be an explanation, and such an explanation was found.

First of all, Jesus was said to have been resurrected. Secondly, the Bible was examined with the purpose of finding what no one had ever seen there before— evidence that the Messiah would be killed without bringing peace to the world or redemption to Israel. (We'll talk about the results of the search—especially Isaiah 53—in a later chapter.) Thirdly, there was the expectation of a second coming, at which time Jesus would carry out the task expected of the Messiah. And finally, there had to be an explanation for the first coming and its catastrophic end. The basic structure of this explanation was to shift the function of the Messiah from a visible level, where it could be tested, to an invisible one, where it could not. The Messiah's goal, at least the first time around, was not the redemption of Israel (which had clearly not taken place) but the atonement for original sin, which was seen as a sort of inner redemption. Whether or not such an atonement was necessary is something we'll discuss later, but at least no one could *see* that it hadn't happened.

Please don't misinterpret this as an argument which describes Jesus' disciples as cynical manipulators of religious beliefs. These are beliefs which resulted from powerful psychological and historical pressures and were surely sincere. But an understanding of the process that formed these beliefs should arouse some skepticism, not about the sincerity with which they were held, but about their truth.

At this point, a little digression of about sixteen hundred years might be helpful in giving us another glimpse of this process. You may have heard about Shabbetai Zevi. He was the most successful Jewish Messiah since the time of Jesus, and in 1666 there were very many Jews throughout the world who believed in him. In September of that year, however, he was forced to become a Moslem, and ten years later he died.

The conversion was as great a shock to Shabbetai Zevi's followers as Jesus' crucifixion was to his. Again, most Jews overcame the need to continue believing and bitterly resigned themselves to yet another disappointment. But others could not, and the similarities between their explanations and those of the early Christians are really striking. (Historians, by the way, generally agree that the basic similarities result mainly from the similarity in the problems faced and not from Christian influence on these seventeenth-century Jews, many of whom lived in Moslem countries.) Shabbetai Zevi was said to have predicted his conversion. He too was expected to return again—first from his converted state and later from beyond the grave. The reality of his death was denied, and here too we find a story about an empty grave. Once again people examined the Bible to find what no one had ever found before—this time, evidence that the Messiah would *convert* without bringing peace to the world or redemption to Israel. And once again they were "successful"; where Christians, for example, found that Isaiah 53 prophesied that the Messiah would be "pierced," Shabbetai's followers found that he would be "profaned." (The word *meholal* in verse 5 can be translated either way.) And finally, there had to be an explanation for the first coming and its catastrophic end. Once more the solution was a shift of the Messiah's function, at least the first time around, from a visible to an invisible level. Here the Messiah had to enter the world of evil to liberate invisible "sparks of holiness," and while we can't go into details here, the explanation is quite as brilliant as its Christian counterpart, if not more so. Eventually, the ultimate step was taken, and Shabbetai Zevi too came to be considered God.

These are both fascinating episodes in the history of religion. In both cases, a Messiah ended his career in a way that made continued belief in him impossible; in both cases, the impossible was made possible by *redefining the role of the Messiah so that it would fit this man's career.*

The Jewish people have refused to take the easy way out. If the Bible's description of the Messiah has not been fulfilled, there is only one conclusion to be reached: he has not yet come. To Jews, who were often subjected to mockery and contempt when asked where their Messiah was, this conclusion was painful, sometimes excruciatingly painful. But an honest facing of the facts made it—and still makes it—inescapable. In adversity and joy, through holocaust and statehood, Jews faithful to the Torah and the prophets can only repeat the words of their forefathers: "I believe with complete faith in the coming of the Messiah, and though he may tarry I shall wait for him every day, hoping that he will come."

3   JESUS AND GOD

The claim that Jesus was the Messiah is one of the beliefs separating Judaism from Christianity. We have explained the Jewish understanding of the Messiah, especially that Judaism never understood the Messiah to be anything more than a human being chosen by God to bring the era of peace and love foretold by the prophets of Israel. We have also explained that Judaism could not accept a reinterpretation of the messianic promise into a purely spiritual state without any historical and political consequences. In short, Judaism understands the redemption as having to occur in the real, political world and not only in the hearts of believers. Since Jesus did not liberate the Jewish people from the Roman yoke and did not end warfare and hatred among individuals and nations, Judaism was not able to accept the messianic claims made for Jesus.

We now come to an even more serious matter. While the question whether Jesus was or was not the Messiah is undoubtedly one of considerable importance, it is hardly comparable in seriousness from the Jewish point of view to the claim that Jesus was God.

Let us first try to understand the Jewish view of God and his relationship to man. From the beginning, the Hebrew Bible (Old Testament) very sharply distinguishes between God and man. God is the creator of heaven and earth, for whom nothing is impossible. Man is a creature of God. He is undoubtedly God's most noble creature, created after all other creatures had been brought into existence. Man is given dominion over all creatures (Genesis 1:28). The most astounding and theologically significant statement is the declaration that man was created in the image and likeness of God (Genesis 1:26–27). Were the difference between God and man anything other than absolute, the statement that man was created in the image of God would hardly have the power it does. It strikes us as one of the Bible's most significant statements because of our prior understanding of the difference between God and man. Given the magnitude of that difference, we are overwhelmed by God's love for man to the extent that a similarity is asserted to connect man with God. The exact meaning of the likeness that obtains between God and man is not easy to define. Nevertheless it is clear that creation in the image of God bestows upon man the unique dignity that he possesses.

But in spite of the dignity of being created in the image of God, it would be a grave error, from the point of view of the Hebrew Bible, to overlook the absolute difference between God and man. It is easy for man to forget the difference. When the serpent tempts Eve (Genesis 3:5), he tells her that if she will eat of the forbidden fruit, "your eyes will be opened and you will be like gods . . . ." A similar theme can be felt in the Tower of Babel incident (Genesis 11:1–9), in which men decide to "build ourselves a city and tower with its top in the heavens, and make a name for ourselves."

Here, as well as in the decision to eat of the forbidden fruit in the Garden of Eden, man aspires to some form of divinity, and invariably this is met by God with the greatest disapproval. Ezekiel (28:2) condemns the prince of Tyre for claiming to be God: "In your arrogance you say, 'I am a god; I sit throned like a god on the high seas.' Yet you are a man and not God, though you consider your thoughts the thoughts of God." In the Hebrew Bible it is essential for man to accept his creaturely status and not to confuse himself with God. Whenever man yields to the temptation to confuse himself with God, he incurs God's anger and is severely punished.

Parallel with man's temptation to confuse himself with God is the horror of the Hebrew Bible at idolatry. Idolatry is the worship of false gods. In the Hebrew Bible only the God of Israel is God. Unlike the other gods of the ancient Near East, the God of Israel is the supreme ruler of the whole universe, so that nowhere can man escape his jurisdiction. The other gods are material creations of man, and to worship them is the worst possible transgression against the creator of the world. The Ten Commandments make this very clear (Exodus 20:2–6). After stating "I am the Lord your God, who brought you out of Egypt, out of the land of slavery," the text continues:

You shall have no other gods to set against me. You shall not make a carved image for yourself nor the likeness of anything in the heavens above, or on the earth below, or in the waters under the earth. You shall not bow down to them or worship them; for I, the Lord your God, am a jealous God. I punish the children for the sins of the fathers to the third and fourth generations of those who hate me. But I keep faith with thousands, with those who love me and keep my commandments.

This passage makes clear the revulsion of God at all material representations of the divine. Any worship directed at a material being, whether created by human artistry or a natural object or living thing, is idolatry. The true God, who created the world and chose the people of Israel, is an invisible God who cannot be contained by anything material. In Deuteronomy 4:15–21 we read:

On the day when the Lord spoke to you out of the fire on Horeb, you saw no figure of any kind; so take good care not to fall into the degrading practice of making figures carved in relief, in the form of a man or a woman, or of any animal on earth or bird that flies in the air, or of any reptile on the ground or fish in the waters under the earth. Nor must you raise your eyes to the heavens and look up to the sun, the moon, and the stars, all the host of the heaven, and be led on to bow down to them and worship them; the Lord your God assigned these to the various peoples under heaven. But you are the people whom the Lord brought out of Egypt, from the smelting furnace, and took for his own possession, as you are to this day.

The finality of God's prohibition against worshipping anything material could not be more clear, whether the object worshipped is a statue or a living animal or a human being.

It is in the light of this that the Christian claim that Jesus was God must be evaluated.

Let us first make clear that this is indeed the claim

that Christianity makes. Sometimes this is overlooked in the heat of discussion. We hear it said that to be a Christian one must accept Jesus as one's personal savior, as the Messiah, and as the Son of God. We have already made clear that in Judaism, and to Jews of the time of Jesus, the Messiah was not God but a human being. The term *Son of God* is often used in the New Testament in connection with Jesus, but this is not an assertion that Jesus was God. The term *Son of God* is used frequently in the Hebrew Bible to refer to the people of Israel (e.g., Deuteronomy 14:1, Isaiah 1:2) or the anointed king of Israel (2 Samuel 7:14, Psalm 2:7, 89:27). In the many instances where *Son of God* occurs in the Hebrew Bible, of which we have given only a small sample above, the term clearly means "elected or chosen by God." By no means does this mean that the people of Israel or the king of Israel is God in any sense. Nevertheless, we cannot escape the fact that classical Christianity asserts that Jesus was God. And it is this claim that makes it so serious for a Jew to embrace Christianity.

How did Christianity come to hold this opinion, which is so deeply unacceptable from the Jewish point of view? It was formally embraced at the Council of Nicaea (325 c.e.), which declared that the Son was "begotten, not made" and "of one essence [*homoousios*] with the Father." This determination was a response to and rejection of the view of Arius, who taught that the Son was a created being who was not of the substance of God and was not eternal. While even for Arius Jesus had certain divine qualities, he was by no means an equal of God but possibly a lower divinity. It is this view that the Council of Nicaea rejected. By speaking of the Son as *homoousios* (of one essence) with the Father, the council took the fateful step of refusing to subordinate Jesus in any sense to his Father, to whom Jesus prays in his last agony on the cross. Both the Son and the Holy Spirit are not creatures of the invisible God of the Hebrew Bible but equal persons with him.

At first glance, this doctrine sounds like an abandonment of monotheism (the teaching that God is one) and a reversion to polytheism (the teaching that there are many gods). The church, however, has traditionally rejected this interpretation and insisted that in spite of the threefold nature of God (Father, Son, and Holy Spirit), each person of which is the full equal of the others, there is also a oneness in God which makes the Christian triune God continuous with the one God of the Hebrew Bible. While the Christian insistence on the oneness of God, in spite of the three co-equal persons in God, is a source of satisfaction to Jews because it keeps Christianity within a monotheistic framework, it must also be said that Judaism finds a "three that are one" doctrine virtually impossible to understand, especially in light of the teaching that only one of these persons became man. It is not our intention to impose a simplistic requirement for "rationality" on religious teachings. Nevertheless, such teachings must be intelligible if they are to be believed, and it is precisely this that is questionable in the teaching of the trinity.

Almost all Jewish scholars and many Christian scholars believe that the doctrine of the full divinity of Jesus is not to be found in the New Testament and would have been abhorrent to the Jew Jesus. There are a number of instances in the New Testament in which we find Jesus himself making almost explicit denials of his divinity. In Luke 18:18–19 we read: "A man of the ruling class put this question to him: 'Good Master, what must I do to win eternal life?' Jesus said to him, 'Why do you call me good? No one is good except God alone." The reply of Jesus makes clear the distinction he draws between himself and God. In Matthew 12:32 Jesus says: "Any man who speaks a word against the Son of Man will be forgiven; but if anyone speaks against the Holy Spirit, for him there will be no forgiveness, either in this age or the age to come," thereby distinguishing between himself and the Holy Spirit. In speaking of the end of days Jesus says (Mark 13:32): "But about that day or about that hour no one knows, not even the angels in heaven, not even the Son; only the Father." One cannot resist asking how the Son and the Father can be equal persons of God when there is knowledge available to the Father that is not available to the Son. It is for these reasons, among others, that it is highly unlikely that Jesus would have found the teaching of his divinity acceptable.

Nevertheless, we should note those elements in the New Testament that made the Nicene development possible. While the Nicene definition almost certainly goes much beyond the New Testament interpretation of the status of Jesus, there are some features of the New Testament view that lay the groundwork for it. Essentially, this has to do with the New Testament view of the person of Jesus. Who was he and how is he related to the figures of the Hebrew Bible?

In the Hebrew Bible, once we leave the Patriarchs,

the key figures are the prophets of Israel, of whom Moses was the first and the greatest. A prophet is a messenger of God. He is sent by God to deliver a message to the people. As a messenger, the prophet does not speak on his own authority but on the authority of the One who sent him. The formula of the prophets is "Thus saith the Lord," and when they utter this phrase they declare themselves to be speaking for the God of Israel, who sent them.

Jesus does not always speak as a messenger of God. While he occasionally refers to the Father who sent him, more often he speaks on his own authority. At times (Matthew 5:21 ff.) he contrasts what "you have been taught" with what "I say unto you," a contrast that the Jewish mind finds most problematic. The question that arises in the mind of the Jewish reader of the New Testament is: Who are you? In all of Judaism it is God who teaches what is right and what is wrong. The prophets, as we have already pointed out, are messengers and spokesmen of God. The rabbis interpret the Written and Oral Law. They have the authority to legislate additions to the Law, but such additions are clearly recognized as rabbinic enactments and cannot contradict God's law. Jesus lays down his own teachings, which he does not attribute to God but to himself. While this does not by itself signify that Jesus was considered God by the New Testament, it does mean that the New Testament attributes a very special status to Jesus beyond that of the prophets depicted in the Hebrew Bible. Occasionally, there are New Testament passages which seem to state the divinity of Jesus more clearly, though these are not passages which report the words of Jesus himself. An example of such a passage would be Colossians 2:9, which asserts that "it is in Christ that the complete being of the Godhead dwells embodied." It should be noted that the Pauline authorship of Colossians has been questioned specifically because of its otherwise un-Pauline Christology.

It is difficult to determine whether the claim that Jesus was God is fully a post–New Testament development or whether it has a firm foundation in the New Testament itself. As we have already said, most Jewish and some Christian scholars believe that the teaching of the divinity of Jesus came into Christianity from gentile sources and was unknown to the original community of the followers of Jesus. Be that as it may, the fact remains that mainline Christianity, since the time of the Council of Nicaea, has adhered to this belief, and it is embraced by those Jews who convert to Christianity. From the Jewish point of view, this belief is idolatrous. The prohibition against idolatry, as we have seen, is one of the most severe in Judaism. According to Jewish law, there are only three transgressions which are so severe that when faced with a choice of transgressing or death, the Jew is commanded to sacrifice his life rather than transgress. One of these is idolatry. It is therefore important for Jews to know that a Jew who believes that Jesus was God in the sense asserted by the Nicene Creed commits idolatry as defined by Jewish law.

There is only one other point to be made. Does a gentile who believes in the divinity of Jesus in accordance with the Nicene Creed commit idolatry? As we will see in Chapter 6, while gentiles are not obligated to obey all the commandments which are obligatory for Jews, one of the commandments which is binding on gentiles is the prohibition against idolatry. From the Jewish point of view, are gentile Christians idolaters? The answer, according to the dominant Jewish view, is that they are not. In Jewish literature, the term that came to be used for the trinitarian concept of God was *shittuf* (partnership). The accepted Jewish view is that belief in *shittuf* does not constitute idolatry for gentiles but does so for Jews. The reason for this is that the definition of what constitutes idolatry is different for Jews and gentiles. Belief in *shittuf,* the belief that God shares his being in equal partnership with Jesus and the Holy Spirit, is not idolatry by the standard of idolatry demanded of gentiles. But the very same belief held by a Jew constitutes idolatry by the standard applicable to Jews. It is for this reason that Judaism does not condemn Christian trinitarianism as idolatry unless those holding the belief are Jews who are bound by the covenant of Sinai.

4 "PROOFS" OF CHRISTIANITY IN THE HEBREW BIBLE

"Jewish Christians" invariably emphasize the existence of proofs in the Hebrew Bible for everything they believe about Jesus. It is this claim which justifies the entire enterprise of "Jewish Christianity," and although it is no longer as fashionable among other Christians as it once was, it really is central to the entire development of Christianity. After all, if the Hebrew Bible is the word of God, it must refer to the most basic religious truths, and we've already seen that without the discovery of a correspondence between the career of Jesus and the Biblical description of the Messiah, the new religion could not have gotten started.

So the Bible was subjected to the most intense scrutiny to make it yield references to beliefs that no one had found there before. We must, of course, examine the results of that effort in some detail, but before we do so, some general observations need to be made.

First of all, anyone whose exposure to the Hebrew Bible has been limited mainly to these "proof-texts" may have been subjected to a serious distortion of perspective. It is terribly important to recognize that these verses are not typical examples of what a person would find by leafing through the Bible. The best of them are rare, isolated, difficult passages, and if their Christian interpretation were true, they would stick out like the proverbial sore thumb in the context of the Bible as a whole. This consideration is logically relevant to the interpretation of individual verses, because it means that there is a heavy burden of proof on a defender of the Christological reading. Let's say that there is a verse which can reasonably be interpreted in two ways. One interpretation would make it fit smoothly into the entire pattern of Biblical religion, while the other would make it say something altogether unexpected and peculiar in the context of the Bible as a whole. It certainly seems more reasonable to chose the first interpretation. As we proceed, we'll see that this consideration becomes relevant in only two or three cases; most of the time the Christological interpretation just doesn't work even without an appeal to the wider context. Still, this is one general point to keep in mind.

There is a second, related observation which is perhaps of even greater importance. When people say that the Hebrew Bible contains references to the trinity, the virgin birth, the divinity of the Messiah, the crucifixion of the Messiah, and other such doctrines, what precisely do they mean? Do they mean that God intended to teach these beliefs clearly and unambiguously to the Jews who lived before Jesus? If so, this is a very difficult position to defend. Not only do Jews fail to see these references, but many modern Christian scholars fail to see them as well. This point will become even more forceful after we discuss the major "proof-texts" in some detail, but it really doesn't require too much documentation. It's unlikely that even representatives of Jewish Christianity will argue that there were Jews in the generation before Jesus who believed in the trinity as a result of references in the Hebrew Bible.

This leaves the possibility that the references to Christian beliefs in the Hebrew Bible are more subtle and can be discerned only by someone who already knows them to be true. Although Jews could not agree to such a claim, it is far more easily defensible than the first possibility, and Christians can argue that the Hebrew Bible has hidden, profound meanings which are accessible once certain truths are already known from other sources. But let us be clear about what this means. It means that the verses we are talking about have a more obvious meaning which does not have anything to do with specifically Christian ideas. It means that they cannot be used to prove these ideas to someone who does not already believe.

This argument is a bit complicated, so let's try to rephrase it more briefly. No one would argue that the Gospels don't contain references to the idea of a virgin birth or the crucifixion of the Messiah, but many reasonable people, including Christians, don't see such references in the Hebrew Bible. If God wanted to teach such ideas clearly in the Hebrew Bible, he could have made them as clear as they are in the Gospels. It seems to follow that God wanted people to be able to read the Bible without seeing these beliefs. In that case, quoting verses to prove these doctrines to non-Christians doesn't appear to make sense. This is a peculiar dilemma, which some medieval Christians solved by saying that the references *are* clear except that God has made the Jews blind. This blindness has now extended to many Christian scholars, and few people today would take such an argument seriously. A Christian might still maintain that the Hebrew Bible contains *indications* (not crystal-clear proofs) of these doctrines, but it should be recognized that this is a much weaker claim than the one usually made in Jewish Christian pamphlets on this subject.

After these preliminary remarks, let us turn to a selection of the central verses used to demonstrate the most important Christian beliefs. Since we can't discuss every single verse in the Hebrew Bible that has ever been quoted in support of Christianity, we are going to choose those passages which are quoted most often and appear most persuasive. In other words, this will be an honest effort to confront the best case that can be presented to demonstrate the truth of Christianity from the Hebrew Bible.

The Trinity

The verses which are supposed to refer to a specifically threefold God are particularly weak as proofs aimed at someone who is not already a Christian. Usually, the argument is simply based on the fact that terms for God appear three times in the verse, and this is just not a persuasive reason for accepting as strange and difficult a doctrine as the trinity. (Needless to say, there are many more verses where terms for God appear only twice, a few verses where they appear more than three times, and an overwhelming majority where such a term appears just once.)

The most commonly cited verse of this sort is "Hear, O Israel, the Lord our God, the Lord is one" (Deuteronomy 6:4). The point is supposed to be that the threefold God ("the Lord our God the Lord") is really one. In fact, however, this is a mistranslation. Since Hebrew omits the present tense of the verb *to be* (even the "is" in "the Lord is one" does not appear in the Hebrew), the correct translation is, "Hear, O Israel, the Lord *is* our God, the Lord is one." Here the trinitarian interpretation can't even get started, but the main point is that this *type* of evidence (from threefold repetition) is significant only for someone who already believes.

The verses said to demonstrate plurality within God that deserve serious attention are supposed to demonstrate such plurality without pointing to a specific number. The passage quoted most frequently to prove this is Genesis 1:26, where God, speaking at the climactic moment in the process of creation, says, "Let us make man in our image." Now, the Bible almost always uses singular verbs in referring to God (beginning in Genesis 1:1), and the plural here really does require explanation. But almost any explanation is superior to the view that the Bible has chosen this verse to teach us the doctrine of the trinity. The verb may be a plural of majesty (the "royal we"), a plural of self-exhortation (as in the English "Let's go" even when someone is talking to himself), or an indication that God was consulting the angels at this critical point of creation. Some Jews have even suggested that God was including the earth in the task of creating man, since it would supply the body while he would supply the soul. (Note that the earth and water were commanded to bring forth other living things—Genesis 1:11, 12, 20, 24.) Every one of these interpretations explains very naturally why the plural verb is used here and not earlier or later in the chapter. Only the trinitarian interpretation fails to do this.

Another verse often cited to demonstrate plurality within God is Psalm 110:1: "The Lord said unto my lord, Sit thou at my right hand until I make thine enemies thy footstool." We are told that the second "lord" should also be capitalized and that one divine being (the Father) was speaking to the other (the Son). It is far more likely, however, that the author of the Psalm is writing a dialogue between God and the author's lord, i.e., the king. Thus, the Lord said to the author's lord (= the king), "Sit at my right hand," i.e., under my protection. ("To David" in the heading of the Psalm means "dedicated to David" and not "by David.") The verse, then, refers to one divine Lord and one human lord and has no reference to plurality within God.

The Virgin Birth

There is only one verse in the entire Hebrew Bible that can be quoted in an attempt to demonstrate that the Messiah—or anyone else—would be born of a virgin. That verse—Isaiah 7:14—reads as follows: "Behold, the *'almah* shall conceive [or "is pregnant"] and shall bear a son, and shall call his name Immanuel."

There are two issues here, and it would be convenient to deal with them separately. (1) Does *'almah* mean virgin? (2) Can the son be Jesus? With respect to the first question, there is no linguistic reason to translate *'almah* as "virgin." The word has a masculine form (*'elem*) which means "young man," and there is every reason to believe that the feminine form means simply "young woman." Just as an *'elem* might or might not have had sexual experience, so an *'almah* might or might not be a virgin.

In fact, among the half-dozen or so times that the word *'almah* appears in the Hebrew Bible, there is an instance in which it is next to impossible for it to refer to a virgin. Proverbs 30:19 speaks of four "ways" or paths: "The way of an eagle in the air, the way of a serpent on a rock, the way of a ship in the sea, and the way of a man with an *'almah*." The common characteristic of these "ways" is apparently that they leave no trace. Such an interpretation is the only one that fits in well with the following verse, which says: "Such is the way of an adulterous woman; she eats and wipes her mouth, and says, 'I have done no wickedness.' " Now, since the one form of intercourse which does leave a trace is "the way of a man" with a virgin, *'almah* here must be a nonvirgin. It should also be kept in mind that whenever the Bible wants to say "virgin" in a legal context, where precision is necessary (Leviticus 21:3, Deuteronomy 22:19, 23:28, Ezekiel 44:22), it always uses the word *betulah*—never *'almah*. Finally, even if we were to concede (against all the evidence) that *'almah* meant "virgin," the verse would mean that this virgin would conceive, and in the process she would lose her virginity. (This is meant quite seriously. Such an interpretation would be a lot more reasonable than the introduction of a radically new doctrine like virgin birth on the basis of this single verse.)

The second question was: Can the son in this verse be Jesus? Isaiah spoke these words to King Ahaz when he was being besieged by two other kings. The prophet wanted to assure him that he needn't worry, and so he told him that this young woman would conceive and have a child, and that "before the child shall know to refuse evil and choose good, the land (of these) two kings shall be forsaken" (Isaiah 7:16).* That the child is Jesus (who was born more than seven hundred years later) is so clearly out of the question that Isaiah 7:14 is really a challenge to the faith of a believing Christian. The question is: How could Matthew (1:22–23) have so grievously misinterpreted Isaiah by referring this verse to Jesus? There might be an answer. Perhaps Isaiah was referring to an event of the near future but subtly hinting at a greater event hundreds of years away. This may be fine for someone who is already a believing Christian, but since it concedes that the plain meaning has nothing to do with Jesus, the verse can no longer be used as proof of the virgin birth.

The Incarnation

At first glance, the belief that the Messiah is God contradicts the repeated Biblical statements that he would be descended from David. The Gospels don't even tell us that Jesus' mother was a descendant of David; instead, in two genealogies that are not quite consistent with one another (Matthew 1:1–16 and Luke 3:23–38), they say this about his *father*. (Jesus himself, despite the Biblical evidence, apparently denied that the

---

* Even though this is not an overt miracle, it is not at all surprising that Isaiah should call it a "sign." Moses himself was given a "sign" which consisted simply of a reassuring prediction that something good would happen in the fairly near future (Exodus 3:12).

Messiah would be descended from David at all—
Matthew 22:41–45 and Mark 12:35–37.) However
these problems are to be resolved, we are told that the
Hebrew Bible says that the Messiah will be God. Let's
see if this is true.

Behold, the days come, says the Lord, that I will raise unto
David a righteous branch, and a king shall reign and pros-
per, and shall execute judgment and justice in the earth.
In his days Judah shall be saved, and Israel shall dwell
safely, and this is the name whereby he shall be called, The
Lord our righteousness (Jeremiah 23:5–6).

If the king is called "The Lord our righteousness," it
would seem that he must be divine. The trouble is that
this is a mistranslation. We've already noted the fact
that Hebrew leaves out the present tense of the verb
to be. What this name really means is "The Lord *is* our
righteousness" (or "salvation"). It doesn't describe
the king as the Lord; rather, like many other symbolic
names in the Bible, it makes a statement about God.
(Even many ordinary Hebrew names like Daniel and
Isaiah are statements about God.) There are, in fact,
almost precise analogies to the structure of this name.
Moses built an altar that he called "The Lord is my
banner" (Exodus 17:15), and Gideon built one that
he called "The Lord is peace" (Judges 6:24). In both
cases the word *is* is missing from the Hebrew, and it is
not necessary to say that no one has ever claimed that
these altars were God.

Now we come to Isaiah 9:5 (9:6 in some translations). The Christological translation of the verse goes
like this: "For a child has been born unto us, a son has

been given to us, and the government has been placed upon his shoulder, and his name shall be called 'wonderful counselor, mighty God, everlasting father, prince of peace.' " A child who is called mighty God and everlasting father would appear to be divine.

Now this is probably the best of all the Christian proof-texts in the Hebrew Bible. The translation just given is linguistically acceptable, and if this verse were found on an isolated scrap of paper produced by an unknown culture, we could legitimately entertain the possibility that this culture believed that God would become a man. It is at this point that we must remember one of the preliminary remarks at the beginning of this chapter. If there is a verse that can reasonably be interpreted in several ways, it doesn't make sense to choose the one which will yield a startling, radical, unique (and, in this case, philosophically difficult) doctrine if the others produce a meaning which fits smoothly into the entire framework of Biblical religion. This is the only verse in the Hebrew Bible which can reasonably be regarded as a reference to a God-man. In light of this, let's take a look at three alternate interpretations.

1. Leave the translation as is, but understand that the "praises" of a king were routinely highly exaggerated in the ancient orient. "Mighty God" means nothing more than "godlike in power" (in fact, the fundamental linguistic meaning of the word translated "God" is probably "powerful one"), and "everlasting father" is the equivalent of the routine greeting, "May the king live forever" (1 Kings 1:31, Nehemiah 2:3).

2. The translation is wrong. After "upon his shoulder," translate: "and the wonderful counselor, the

mighty God, the eternal father [i.e., God] has called his name 'prince of peace.' " In this translation, "mighty God" and "everlasting father" are not part of the child's name at all.

3. The strongest likelihood is that both translations given so far are wrong. We have already seen that symbolic names in the Bible tend to be complete sentences that often make a statement about God ("The Lord is our righteousness," "The Lord is my banner," "The Lord is peace"). The same section of Isaiah contains three symbolic names which are complete sentences: "A remnant will return" (Isaiah 7:3), "God is with us" (Isaiah 7:14—that's the meaning of *Immanuel*), "Speed spoil hasten plunder" (Isaiah 8:3). It is likely, therefore, that this name is also a complete sentence and that it makes a statement about God (not directly about the child). Translate the name as follows (the grammatical structure is perfectly acceptable): "The mighty God, the eternal father, the prince of peace is planning a wondrous deed." (If you know Hebrew, the point is that *el gibbor avi 'ad sar shalom* is the subject of *yo'etz*.) The child is probably Hezekiah, and the wondrous deed is the destruction of Sennacherib's army. In any case, the verse does not speak of a divine or everlasting son.

Finally, there is one more verse on the divinity of the Messiah which serves double duty by demonstrating his birth in Bethlehem as well. "And thou, Bethlehem Ephratah, though thou be little among the thousands of Judah, yet out of thee shall come forth unto me one who is to be a ruler in Israel, whose origins are of old, from days of yore" (Micah 5:1 = 5:2 in some translations). The Christological translation of the last phrase (*miqedem mimei 'olam*) is "of old, from everlasting," which demonstrates that this ruler is eternal and hence divine. But aside from the almost immediate reference to "the Lord his God," we are once again dealing with a mistranslation. The crucial words appear in another verse, where they cannot possibly refer to eternity: "Then shall the offering of Judah and Jerusalem be pleasant unto the Lord as in days of old, and as in former years" (*kimei 'olam u-keshanim qadmoniyyot* —Malachi 3:4).

The point of the phrase is that this future ruler, who may indeed be the Messiah, will have come forth from Bethlehem because his royal origins are "of old, from days of yore," i.e., from the old and venerable House of David, *and David was born in Bethlehem*. In other words, according to the most probable reading of this verse, it not only fails to say that the Messiah is everlasting, it doesn't even say that he will be born in Bethlehem. The point is that Bethlehem will be his indirect point of origin because it was the birthplace of the father of his dynasty. Jews don't have to insist on this last point; the Messiah may very well be born in Bethlehem. It's just that the verse probably doesn't say this.

Finally, we cannot avoid at least some reference to the historical question of Jesus' actual birthplace. Since this is a delicate question and it is not our purpose to engage in historical criticism of the Gospels, it might be best to note briefly the view expressed by Father Raymond Brown, who has written the most comprehensive study of the infancy stories in Matthew and Luke. He begins by quoting another scholar's remark that "the overwhelming evidence to the contrary has made the thesis that Bethlehem was *not* the historical birthplace of Jesus the accepted opinion of New Testament scholarship." Father Brown considers this statement too strong, but he goes on to speak of the "grave objections against the claim that [birth at Bethlehem is] a historical fact" and concludes that "the evidence for birth at Bethlehem is much weaker than the evidence" for other elements of the infancy narratives (*The Birth of the Messiah* [1977]), pp. 513-516). While this is not the place to discuss the difficulties which lead to this conclusion, it is certainly the view of most New Testament scholars that the tradition that Jesus was born in Bethlehem is at least uncertain and that it may have arisen *as a result* of one interpretation (probably erroneous) of Micah 5:1. (Matthew 2:5–6 specifically makes the connection.) If so (and we are not insisting that this view is firmly proven), not only does Micah 5:1 not predict Jesus' birth, the story of Jesus' birth in Bethlehem may have arisen as a result of Micah 5:1.

To sum up: 1. The verse does not speak of an everlasting ruler.
2. It probably does not speak of the ruler's birth in Bethlehem.
3. Jesus may not have been born in Bethlehem.
4. Even if points 2 and 3 are wrong, this would not demonstrate that Jesus was the Messiah. When the Messiah comes, he may indeed turn out to have been born in Bethlehem.

The Humiliating Death of the Messiah

We are now ready to take a careful look at what is supposed to be the most impressive proof-text of them all: Isaiah 52:13–53:12. The passage describes a "servant of the Lord" who will suffer from (or for) the sins of others, "place his grave among the wicked," and "see his seed and live a long life." Now, this was probably the most important passage found by early Christians struggling with the paradox of the crucifixion, and the idea that Jesus died for the sins of others probably originates from this chapter. In other words, it is not that Jesus' death for the sins of others is a remarkable fulfillment of Isaiah 53; it is because of Isaiah 53 that people attributed this purpose to Jesus' death. In a way, the point is even clearer in this case than it was when we made a similar point about Micah 5:1. In that case, either Jesus was born in Bethlehem or he was not. Here, no one saw Jesus die for the sins of others; they only saw him die. The interpretation of his death is a result, not a striking fulfillment, of Isaiah 53. We must be careful not to get caught in circular reasoning.*

Actually, before getting involved in such problems, we have to ask ourselves the most basic questions of

---

* We should also recognize the possibility that the problem of circular reasoning in these proof-texts is even more extensive than we've indicated so far. After all, once Christians interpreted Isaiah 53 and Psalm 22 as descriptions of the crucifixion, it was natural for them to *assume* that all the minute details in those chapters must have been fulfilled. The stories of the crucifixion would then be elaborated to include such details (e.g., Jesus' silence before his accusers, the casting of lots for his garments, etc.). It is very likely that there was precisely this development of legendary detail, and we should not allow ourselves to be misled by it.

all: Who is "the servant of the Lord"? Do we have any reason to think that he is the Messiah? One way of trying to answer these questions is to see if the term *servant of the Lord* appears elsewhere in Isaiah where the identification might be clear. Another way is to examine Isaiah 53 itself and see whether or not the descriptions of the "servant" there give us any reason to identify him with the Messiah.

With respect to the first approach, we are rather lucky, because a servant of the Lord is mentioned in eight chapters between Isaiah 41 and 50. In five of the chapters, the servant is clearly and unambiguously the people of Israel (41:8–9; 44:1, 2, 21, 26; 45:4, 48:20; 49:3 [49:5 is problematical and could be either Israel or the prophet, depending on the translation]). One reference is probably to the prophet (50:10); the references in the other two chapters are uncertain (42:1, 2, 19, 21, 26; 43:10), but they can easily refer to Israel (compare 42:19 with 43:8). What all this means is that when we get to Isaiah 52–53, we should be strongly predisposed to regard any "servant of the Lord" as the people of Israel. To say that the servant in Isaiah 53 is the Messiah, we would need extraordinarily persuasive reasons. Instead of such persuasive reasons, we have no reasons at all.

How do we go about deciding whether a particular Biblical passage refers to the Messiah? Well, we've already seen that *Messiah* is simply another way of saying "the king of the house of David who will rule over a redeemed Israel in an age of peace, prosperity, and justice." There is nothing—absolutely nothing—in Isaiah 53 to indicate that the servant is this king. Incredibly, this is really all that needs to be said about Isaiah 53 as a Christian proof-text.*

Nevertheless, the chapter has become so central that a few more remarks are necessary. We have seen that our most reasonable expectation ought to be that the servant is the Jewish people. As a collective symbol, the servant can be said to suffer any fate suffered by many individual Jews, and he can be said to enjoy the rewards of any large number of Jews. Hence, although the prophet makes no mention of an intervening resurrection, the servant can go to his grave (because of the martyrdom of so many Jews) and later "see his seed and live a long life."

So far, we have been arguing that any Messianic interpretation of Isaiah 53 is improbable. It's time to note that a specifically Christian reading is even more difficult. First of all, whatever the complex relationship between the "Father" and the "Son" might be, is it really reasonable for God to call himself his own servant? If not for this chapter in Isaiah, would a believer in the trinity even consider the use of such an inappropriate term? Secondly, a straightforward reading of "see his seed and live a long life" doesn't fit either the first coming or the second, since no Christian expects Jesus to have children, and "long life" does not normally mean "eternal life." A forced, nonliteral understanding of "seed" and "long life" becomes the

---

* The fact that some Talmudic rabbis took the chapter messianically (though not in the Christian sense) is of interest to historians, but it does not mean that Jews are in any way obligated to adopt such an interpretation. By the Middle Ages, virtually every Jewish authority rejected it, not only because of opposition to Christianity, but because there is no basis for it in the text.

only way out. Thirdly, the Hebrew phrase *ish makh'o-vot vidua' holi* ("a man of pains, and familiar with ill-ness") refers to a man of constant, long-lasting afflic-tions and cannot refer to anguish, however intense, which lasted but a few hours, or even days. Finally, the lack of any explicit reference to a resurrection makes a Christological reading all the more difficult. In other words, even though parts of the crucifixion story may well have been written with Isaiah 53 in mind, there remains a residue of material in that chap-ter which cannot be squared with Jesus' career or with the later belief that he was divine. Isaiah's "suffering servant" is the Jewish people, and it is a terrible irony that their sufferings through the ages were made even more intense because of the belief that they are the villains, rather than the victims, in Isaiah 53.*

We could go on to deal with other verses that have been quoted to support Christian doctrines. The seventy weeks of Daniel, for example, don't really culminate in the time of Jesus, and the seventieth week in particular works out so poorly that even the most ingenious calculations require the assumption that God granted the Jews a last-minute delay of several decades. There is no reason to believe that Psalm 22 refers to the Messiah, and the translation "They pierced my hands and feet" (Psalm 22:17) is not based on the standard Hebrew text. We're afraid, however, that this

---

* We should note that some scholars consider the servant to be the prophet. This view requires us to take the verses about his death as references to his going to the brink of death, and there are Biblical parallels to such a usage. Although we think that the "Israel" interpretation is correct, the "prophet" interpretation is more easily defensible than the Messianic one.

chapter has already gotten too long, and we've dealt in some detail with the most important verses. The central point is that the intense effort to turn the Hebrew Bible into a Christian book just doesn't work. The Bible must therefore be read as it really is—as a purely Jewish work. Jews who become interested in Jewish Christianity are often led for the first time to revere the Hebrew Bible as the product of divine inspiration. We ask such people to retain that reverence, not as Jewish Christians, but simply as Jews.

5   THE FORGIVENESS OF SIN

Contemporary Christianity appears in various forms. While there was a time when almost all Christian churches were engaged in missionizing Jews, in recent times most churches have discontinued special efforts directed at Jews. There are various reasons for this change. One of the most significant is the widespread conviction among many Christian thinkers that Judaism stands in a special relationship to Christianity and, therefore, that Jews cannot be addressed as people in need of salvation. Thus, the great contemporary Protestant theologian Karl Barth, speaking of the people of Israel, wrote:

For it is incontestable that this people as such is the holy people of God: the people with whom God has dealt in His grace and in His wrath; in the midst of whom He has blessed and judged, enlightened and hardened, accepted and rejected; whose cause either way He has made His own, and has not ceased to make His own, and will not cease to make His own. They are all of them by nature sanctified by Him, sanctified as ancestors and kinsmen of the Holy One in Israel, in a sense that Gentiles are not by nature, not even the best of Gentiles, not even the Gentile Christians, not even the best of Gentile Christians, in spite of the fact that they too are now sanctified by the Holy One of Israel and have become Israel (*Church Dogmatics,* II, 2, p. 287).

But there are Christians who see things otherwise. Most "Jewish Christian" groups in this country preach a straightforward "Jesus or damnation" theology. Jews coming into contact with these groups are told that if they do not accept Jesus as their personal savior, they are condemned to the tortures of everlasting hell since their sins cannot be forgiven. They are also told that sin can be forgiven only by the shedding of blood, and since Judaism no longer practices sacrifice, it cannot bring about the forgiveness of sin. What can be said about this point of view?

First of all, we must ask whether the simple "Jesus or damnation" point of view is indeed authentic Christian teaching. In the final analysis, we must let Christians answer this question, though noting that a very large segment of Christianity does not accept the view that all those who deny Jesus as savior are condemned to everlasting hell. At the same time, it must be conceded that the New Testament attributes to Jesus statements that sound very much like the "Jesus or damnation" teaching. As an example, Jesus is quoted in Mark 16:16–18 as saying:

Go forth to every part of the world, and proclaim the Good News to the whole creation. Those who believe it and receive baptism will find salvation; those who do not believe will be condemned. Faith will bring with it these miracles: believers will cast out devils in my name and speak in strange tongues; if they handle snakes or drink any deadly poison, they will come to no harm; and the sick on whom they lay their hands will recover.

Because it is difficult to insist that believing Christians are immune to the harmful effects of snakebites or deadly poisons, many Christians have found it necessary to interpret these passages more spiritually and less literally. And once that is done, it is equally possible to give a more merciful reading to the "Jesus or damnation" segment of the quotation. But some Christians have refused to take this path and, basing themselves on passages such as the one quoted, they have offered a stark choice between faith in Jesus and eternal damnation. For Jews, the view that the six million victims murdered by the Nazis went directly from Hitler's ovens to eternal hell-fire is morally offensive. It must be noted that the certainty of damnation without faith in Jesus is understood not as a function of the individual's sin but rather as a fate preordained by the sin of Adam, whose fall and guilt are carried by all human beings at birth, making them worthy of hell even before they have had a chance to sin at all.

Judaism, too, takes sin very seriously. From the beginning, the Hebrew Bible documents man's recurring disobedience to the commands of God and the punishments meted out to him as a result of his disobedience. It is true that Judaism does not interpret the sin of Adam to mean that every subsequent human being starts his career with the verdict of guilty entered against him. Nevertheless, the Bible, as well as subsequent Jewish history, shows that sin is an ever-present human temptation to which we succumb far too often. The prophets of Israel interpret the various calamities that befall the people of Israel as the result of the people's sin. Similarly, the rabbis interpreted the destruction of the Second Temple in 70 C.E. as resulting from Israel's sin.

It is further true that sacrifice plays an important role in the forgiveness of sin. The Temple in Jerusalem, built on the spot where Abraham prepared to sacrifice his son Isaac until commanded, at the last moment, not to do so, was and remains the holiest spot on earth for Jews. It is plain to any reader of the Pentateuch that God commanded a whole system of sacrifices to play a role in the atonement of sin. Because this is so, there is no doubt that the destruction of the Temple in 70 C.E. (not to speak of the earlier destruction) was a great problem for Judaism. What effect would the discontinuation of the sacrifices have on Israel's relationship with God? Could sins be forgiven without sacrifices? Could Judaism survive in exile, without a Temple and with Jews living in many different countries?

Before going any further, we must now speak of the traditional Christian explanation of how the death of Jesus took the place of the sacrifices offered in the Temple so that no further Temple sacrifice has been needed since this final sacrifice. This view is most clearly expressed in Hebrews 9:13–14, where we are told:

For if the blood of goats and bulls and the sprinkled ashes of a heifer have power to hallow those who have been defiled and restore their external purity, how much greater is the power of the blood of Christ, a spiritual and eternal sacrifice; and his blood will cleanse our conscience from the deadness of our former ways and fit us for the service of the living God.

The argument is that the sacrifices brought in the Temple had only limited efficacy because they had to be repeated periodically, while the death as a sacrifice of Jesus was perfect and was therefore the sacrifice to end all sacrifice.

Judaism rejects this view on simple grounds. The God of Israel forbids human sacrifice. Again and again, in the Hebrew Bible, God condemns the sacrificing of children to Moloch with particular vehemence (e.g., Leviticus 18:21, 20:2–5 among others). While God's command to Abraham to sacrifice Isaac perhaps established in principle God's right to demand human sacrifice, his last-minute intervention established his firm desire that not human beings but animals be sacrificed to him. Once this is grasped, it becomes impossible for the faith of Israel to accept the account of a human sacrifice as conforming to the will of God. It can be argued that the death of Jesus was not a sacrifice in the sense in which human sacrifice is forbidden, since it was voluntary on his part and those who killed him did not do so for the sake of bringing a sacrifice. But if that is so, then the death of Jesus can only be considered a sacrifice metaphorically and cannot substitute for, and certainly cannot terminate, the sacrifices specifically commanded by God in the Hebrew Bible. Many Jews and Christians see the reestablishment of the State of Israel as the beginning of the redemption of the Jewish people as foretold by the prophets of Israel. These same prophets foretold the rebuilding of the Temple and the resumption of the sacrifices (e.g.,

Zechariah 14:21, Isaiah 60:7, Malachi 3:1–4), a resumption for which traditional Jews have prayed since the time of the destruction. These prophecies in themselves indicate that the Hebrew Bible never envisioned any event that would make the reestablishment of the sacrifices in Jerusalem unnecessary, and if this is so, then the death of Jesus cannot be considered the sacrifice to end all sacrifice.

Nevertheless, the seriousness of sin and the need for its forgiveness remain. For the Christian mind, this is accomplished by the death of Jesus. How does Judaism deal with this problem?

It does so through the idea of repentance. It is the basic teaching of God in the Hebrew Bible that God does not will the death of the wicked but their repentance (Jeremiah 18:1–10). Ezekiel 18:21–23 expresses this most clearly:

It may be that a wicked man gives up his sinful ways and keeps all my laws, doing what is just and right. That man shall live; he shall not die. None of the offenses he has committed shall be remembered against him; he shall live because of his righteous deeds. Have I any desire, says the Lord God, for the death of a wicked man? Would I not rather that he should mend his ways and live?

Repentance involves recognizing that one has done wrong, being sorry for having done so, and asking God sincerely to forgive one's sins. Any Jew who does so will be forgiven by God.

Many scholars consider repentance a higher and more spiritual relationship to God than the offering of sacrifice. Frequently, the great prophets of the Hebrew

Bible criticized those who brought sacrifices while continuing their evil deeds (e.g., Amos 5:21–22). The conclusion that these scholars draw from the prophetic denunciations of sacrifice without repentance (repentance not only means saying you're sorry, but also changing your conduct) was that the prophets considered sacrifice primitive and unnecessary. The truth is that the prophets denounced sacrifice without repentance, but they deeply respected sacrifice combined with repentance. The prophets had the highest respect for the Temple and its divinely ordained sacrifices, and expressed great sadness about the time after the exile when Israel could no longer fulfill its sacrificial obligations (Hosea 9:4).

But that time came, and while we reject the view that the prophets considered sacrifice unnecessary even while the Temple stood, we cannot overlook the emphasis that the prophets laid on repentance. It is perhaps in Psalm 51:18–21 that the matter is best summed up. The Psalm starts with the expression of a sense of sin which weighs heavily on the writer. He begs God to cleanse him of his sin and then continues:

For thou delightest not in a sacrifice that I would bring; thou hast no pleasure in burnt offering. The sacrifices of God are a broken spirit; a broken and a contrite heart, O God, Thou wilt not despise. Do good in thy favor unto Zion; built thou the walls of Jerusalem. Then wilt thou delight in the sacrifices of righteousness, in burnt offering and whole offering; then will they offer bullocks upon thine altar.

When sacrifice is possible it is necessary, though useless without repentance (the "broken spirit" and "wounded heart"). When sacrifice is not possible, God forgives those who sincerely repent.

Judaism thus looks to God for forgiveness. In his infinite mercy God waits for man's return to him, and when this happens, God forgives all his sins. The rabbis taught that not only are the sins of a repentant sinner forgiven, but they are turned into virtuous deeds. So great is the power of repentance.

6 ON JEWS, GENTILES, AND "JEWISH CHRISTIANS"

Several times in the course of our discussion of Judaism and Christianity we have distinguished between Jews and gentiles. At the outset, we emphasized that this booklet is directed in part at Jews who are thinking of converting to Christianity. In the chapter dealing with the divinity of Jesus, we explained that for a Jew to believe that Jesus was God constitutes idolatry, while the same trinitarian belief is not idolatry when held by a gentile. These points may have raised certain questions. What is a Jew, and how is he different from a gentile? Are different things expected from Jews and gentiles? What is the meaning of the Law (Torah), and are only Jews supposed to obey it or is everyone so obligated?

Most religions consist of a set of teachings dealing with right conduct and man's obligations to God or the gods. Membership in these religions is generally open to anyone who subscribes to the teachings of the religion and endeavors to live in accordance with them. In fact, not only is such membership open to all, but great efforts are often made to attract people to the religion in question. Such missionary efforts are made because these religions believe themselves to be in possession of important truths which they wish to bring to the attention of all, and often because they teach that salvation depends on the acceptance of their belief.

In this respect, Judaism is different. It believes itself to be the religion of the Jewish people, with its teachings obligatory only for Jews. Judaism believes that at Mount Sinai God gave Moses the teachings contained in the Pentateuch (Five Books of Moses), which regulate the life of the Jew. The Pentateuch contains teachings which deal with every aspect of human life, ranging from the ethical to commandments and prohibitions that regulate our diet, sex lives, and ritual observances. These commandments, traditionally said to be 613 in number, exist in written form in the Pentateuch and are elaborated in the Oral Law, which was also revealed to Moses at Sinai but orally rather than in writing. Later these oral teachings were written down, and these writings are called the Talmud. Together, the Written and Oral Law have guided Jewish life for over two thousand years.

But why is there a special set of laws which are binding only for Jews and not for gentiles? The answer is found in the Bible. There we are told that God selected Abraham as his particular servant, promising that his descendants would become a great people who would be God's particular people (Genesis 12:1–3). And here we come to the crux of the matter, which is Israel's election, a doctrine that many people over the ages have found difficult to fathom. Isn't God the father of all? Doesn't he love all nations equally? If there is any group that God prefers, wouldn't it be the group con-

sisting of all those who love God and deal justly with
their fellows, no matter what nation these good people
come from?

From our human point of view, this does sound like
the fairer way of proceeding. But it is not what the Bible
tells us God did. He chose Abraham as his beloved and
the descendants of Abraham as the nation of God.
Whatever God's reasons for choosing Abraham, the
people of Israel, once chosen, thereby becomes the elect
people of God from whom God demands a code of
conduct far more stringent than that demanded of
anyone else. That is why the Torah is binding only for
Jews. But is a person a Jew if he does not obey all of
the Torah? From the Jewish point of view, whether
someone is a Jew is determined by his mother: if a
mother is Jewish, so are her children. Whether they are
good Jews depends on the extent to which they obey
God's commandments. But the election of Abraham
is an election of his seed, and it is therefore physical
descent that determines membership in the Jewish people. If your mother was Jewish, so are you, no matter
what you believe. It is, of course, true that conversion
to Judaism is possible. But it has generally been discouraged in Judaism. Why?

The answer is that Judaism believes all good people
to have a share in the world to come. In order to clarify
this, we must now speak of the Noachide laws. As we
have already seen, the Torah and its 613 commandments are intended only for Jews. How, then, is a gentile to live? Does God not care how gentiles act, or does
he make demands of gentiles as well as Jews? Judaism
teaches that God does indeed make demands of gentiles, though they are different from those he makes of

Jews. The Talmud speaks of the laws that are binding for gentiles as the Noachide commandments, basing itself on Genesis 9:1–17. There God makes a covenant with Noah never again to cause a flood to come upon the world. At the same time God demands of Noah and his descendants not to take human life (Genesis 9:6), and the rabbis include other aspects of moral law, such as theft, adultery and incest, idolatry, etc. Judaism believes that a gentile who obeys the Noachide commandments has a place in the world to come. This is the basic reason why conversion to Judaism by gentiles is discouraged. A gentile who wishes to convert to Judaism is told that, as a gentile, he can find favor with God by adhering to the Noachide commandments. Were he to convert, he would be obligated to fulfill all the commandments of the Torah, and since this is a difficult thing to do, he is advised to stay with the Noachide covenant, under which it is easier to please God. Should a gentile persist in his desire to become a Jew, he must indicate his willingness to accept all the commandments of the Torah. He is then circumcised and miraculously becomes a Jew with all the obligations of a Jew.

Now that we have discussed the Jewish teaching on the obligations of Jews and gentiles, we can inquire as to the Christian point of view on this matter. Here matters become somewhat complicated. There is what might be called the traditional Christian teaching, and there is the teaching that emerges from a more careful reading of Christian sources.

The traditional Christian teaching has been that with the coming of Jesus as the Messiah, all differences between Jews and gentiles are erased (Galatians

3:28). The Law was obligatory only until the coming of Jesus. With his coming the Law is no longer binding. The Jew who has faith in Jesus can stop obeying the Law. He can marry a gentile, so that within two or three generations all Jewish identity is lost, and this is indeed what has happened throughout the centuries to Jews who entered the church. Needless to say, Judaism considers a Jew's severance of his bonds with the Jewish people a tragedy. It is the faith of Israel that the election of this people is eternal and irrevocable, and that the Law remains obligatory for all Jews for all times.

A more careful reading of various passages in the New Testament indicates that what has been described as the traditional Christian teaching may not be the original teaching of the early church. In Acts 15 we read of the Jerusalem Council, which discussed whether gentile converts to Christianity need be circumcised and obey the Law. The decision rendered was that they need not embrace the whole Torah, only the Noachide commandments (Acts 15:20–21). The very fact that the question whether gentiles who embraced Jesus needed to obey the Law could be discussed at length indicates rather clearly that there was unanimous agreement that Jews who believed in Jesus were obligated to continue obeying the Law. If this is so, the intention of the early church was for a church with two branches, the Jewish and the gentile. They would have their faith in Jesus in common but would differ in that Jews would remain under the commandments of the Torah while gentiles would be bound by the Noachide laws. If this is so, then the original Christian view of how Jews who have faith in Jesus ought to behave is quite different from traditional Christian teaching.

In recent years various groups have come into being that consider themselves "Jewish Christians." They preach Jesus as their savior, yet seem intent on maintaining a form of Jewish identity. What is the Jewish reaction to such groups?

We have already explained why Judaism rejects the belief that Jesus was the Messiah. But the claims of these groups to Jewish identity are made even more dubious by the fact that they are generally quite unclear about their commitment to Jewish practices and even Jewish survival. Some of them practice various Jewish customs, such as wearing *tsitsit* (fringes) and lighting candles on Friday nights. But do they believe that a Jew is obligated to obey the whole Torah? Do they believe that Jews must only marry other Jews, or do they believe, because of their faith in Jesus, that intermarriage with gentiles is permitted? In short, do they believe that it is the will of God that the seed of Abraham remain in the world as an identifiable people chosen by God? There is very little reason to think that they do. In fact, their primary identification seems to be with gentile, evangelical Christianity. As such, it is to be expected that the traditional pattern will be repeated. The descendants of Jews who come to believe in Jesus as the Messiah will disappear as Jews within two or three generations. And that is clearly not the will of God.

A Jew attracted to "Jewish Christianity" must ask himself whether he is willing to contribute to the dissolution of the Jewish people. If the group he joins consists of Jews and gentiles, if this group does not consider the commandments of the Torah binding on Jews, if it can be expected that Jews in this group will gradually be absorbed into the larger, gentile Christian community, then such a Jew is opting for the dissolution of the people God wants to remain his eternal people. It is imperative that Jews know this.

Furthermore, every form of "Jewish Christianity" in existence today teaches Jesus as God and not only as the Messiah. Any Jew who embraces this belief commits idolatry. While he does not thereby cease to be a Jew, since a Jew always remains a Jew, he commits one of the gravest sins of which a Jew is capable. It is imperative that Jews know this.

A FINAL WORD

In this booklet we have tried, sincerely and respect-
fully, to explain the Jewish point of view concerning
Jews who have embraced or are thinking of embracing
Christianity. In the final analysis, it is you who must
make the decision.

In the course of our discussions, we have concen-
trated on the major theological issues. Could Jesus
have been the Messiah? What is the Jewish conception
of God? Does the Hebrew Bible demonstrate the truth
of Christianity? How does God forgive sins? Is devotion to "Jewish Christianity" consistent with a commitment to the survival of the Jewish people? We have
tried to show that the arguments for your conversion
are not persuasive on an intellectual level.

In a decision of this magnitude, however, there are
emotional factors involved as well—and there is nothing wrong with that. You may have felt them in the
form of a sense of fellowship and genuine religious
concern on the part of your Christian friends. But you
have also felt the instinctive opposition of many Jews
to the prospect of your conversion, and it is worth
considering the reasons for that opposition.

You were born a Jew because your ancestors clung

to their faith. Often, they had to give their very lives when misguided Christians forced the choice of baptism or death on them. You were born a Jew because your ancestors had the supreme courage to choose death. Had they chosen baptism, you would not have been born a Jew. Their readiness to make the ultimate sacrifice creates a special obligation for their descendants not to render that sacrifice meaningless. Before abandoning the Judaism of your ancestors, you must make an all-out effort to study it, to know it, to live it.

In the early part of this century, a Jewish philosopher named Franz Rosenzweig was on the verge of converting to Christianity. He had been brought up in a fairly assimilated Jewish home in which Judaism played a very small part. But feeling he should convert as a Jew and not as a pagan, he decided to attend a Yom Kippur (Day of Atonement) service in a small traditional synagogue in Berlin. The spirit and liturgy of the day transformed his life. He came to know that God wanted Jews to remain Jews, to be faithful to the covenant God had made with the Patriarchs. Franz Rosenzweig became one of the great Jewish thinkers of our time.

The people of Israel was chosen by God to be "a nation of priests and a holy people" (Exodus 19:6). By remaining loyal to your people, you can help it live up to its divine calling. By considering the devotion of its martyrs throughout the ages, and by remembering the fate of the six million who were murdered in our own time because they were Jews, you can come to live a life worthy of their sacrifice.

You are facing a critically important decision. Your choice will determine not only your own religious destiny, but the identity of your descendants as well. Study intensively, consider carefully, and—with the help of God—choose wisely.

SUGGESTIONS FOR FURTHER READING

1. Berger, David. *The Jewish-Christian Debate in the High Middle Ages: A Critical Edition of the Niẓẓahon Vetus with an Introduction, Translation and Commentary.* Philadelphia: Jewish Publication Society, 1978.

    The introduction and commentary present a history and analysis of almost all the major arguments from the beginnings of Christianity through the thirteenth century.

2. Braude, Morris. *Conscience on Trial.* New York: Exposition Press, 1962.

    Translations of the major medieval disputations in Paris, Barcelona, and Tortosa.

3. Buber, Martin. *Two Types of Faith.* New York: Harper, 1961.

    A study that attributes the break between the two religions primarily to Paul.

4. Friedlander, Gerald. *The Jewish Sources of the Sermon on the Mount.* Rev. Ed., New York: Ktav, 1969.

    On the ethical teachings of Jesus and Judaism.

5. Kimhi, Joseph. *The Book of the Covenant.* Trans. by Frank Talmage. Toronto: Pontifical Institute of Medieval Studies, 1972.

    One of the earliest Jewish polemics against Christianity.

6. Lasker, Daniel. *Jewish Philosophical Polemics against Christianity in the Middle Ages.* New York: Ktav; Anti-Defamation League, 1977.

    An analysis of the medieval Jewish assertions that the doctrines of trinity, incarnation, and transubstantiation involve logical contradictions.

7. Neubauer, Adolf and Driver, S. R. *The Fifty-third Chapter of Isaiah According to the Jewish Interpreters*. New York: Ktav, 1969, 2 vols.

    Jewish commentaries on one of the central Christian "proof-texts."

8. Parkes, James. *Judaism and Christianity*. Chicago: Univ. of Chicago Press, 1948.

    A Christian scholar's views of the two religions.

9. Rankin, Oliver Shaw. *Jewish Religious Polemic of Earlier and Later Centuries*. New York: Ktav, 1970.

    Translations of several Jewish polemical texts.

10. Silver, Abba Hillel. *Where Judaism Differed*. Philadelphia: Jewish Publication Society, 1957.

    Concentrates on the distinctive characteristics of Judaism.

11. Talmage, Frank, ed. *Disputation and Dialogue: Readings in the Jewish-Christian Encounter*. New York: Ktav; Anti-Defamation League, 1975.

    A source book.

12. Troki, Isaac. *Faith Strengthened*. Trans. by M. Mocatta. New York: Ktav, 1970.

    A sixteenth-century polemic which became a standard work.